D1391958

CHUB : 10 lbs 8 ozs
Place : River Annan,
Dumfries-shire
Date : 1955

DACE : 1 lb 8 ozs 5 drms
Place : River Avon, Hampshire
Date : 1932

EEL : 8 lbs 8 ozs
Place : Bitteswell Lake
Date : 1922

GRAYLING : 7 lbs 2 ozs
Place : River Melgum,
Aberdeenshire
Date : 1949

PERCH : 5 lbs 15 ozs 6 drms
Place : River Stour, Essex
Date ; 1949

GUDGEON : 4 ozs 4 drms
Place ; River Soar, Leicestershire
Date ; 1950

PIKE
47 lbs 11 ozs
Place ; Loch Lomond,
Scotland
Date ; 1945

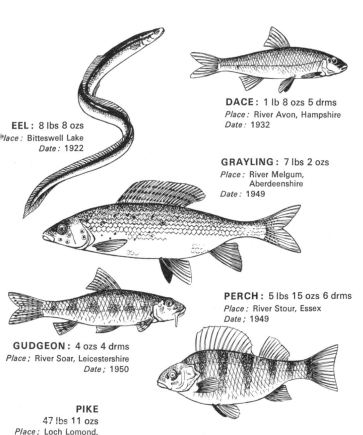

A Ladybird Book
Series 633

Angling is one of the most popular of hobbies. Nowadays, some people say it is pointless because anglers no longer kill and take home their catch. They return it alive to the water. But ask any angler WHY he does it, and in no uncertain terms he will tell you the reasons. We hope you will have discovered these reasons by the end of this book.

Note: It is wise to learn to swim before you fish any waters, otherwise you may put other people in danger as well as yourself.

Coarse Fishing

by N. SCOTT

with illustrations by B. H. ROBINSON

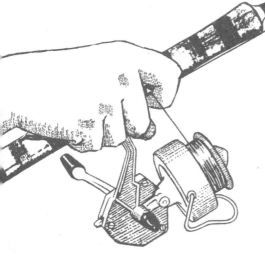

Publishers : Wills & Hepworth Ltd Loughborough

First published 1969   *Printed in England*

Coarse Fishing

Fishing for coarse fish, using a rod and line, is a hobby for all ages. It takes skill to 'play' any fish, large or small. Anglers have to learn this skill. An angler must also have a knowledge of the water in which he fishes, an understanding of the life and habits of the fish in it, and the ability to identify the various species of fish.

Coarse fish is the name given to any fish living in rivers, lakes, ponds and canals, other than Salmon, Trout and Sea-Trout.

Before fishing in *any* waters, you must be sure that you are allowed to do so. There are some stretches of water, but not many, that are free to any anglers, particularly children. So first you must buy a licence from your local River Board. It may also be necessary to obtain fishing permission from the owner of the land fronting the water, or from the Club holding the fishing rights.

It is breaking the law to fish on any water without a licence; but the cost of a rod licence is cheap, and the charges for a day's fishing in most inland waters are also low. To find out how to get a licence and fishing permit, go to any fishing-tackle dealer. He will also tell you about any angling clubs in the district. Most of these clubs have junior sections. Many youth organisations and schools also have their own angling clubs, so there is plenty of advice and help available to you.

Fees received by River Boards and angling clubs are used to help the angler by maintaining the waters and restocking them with fresh fish when necessary.

Angling Clubs

All hobbies and organisations have rules to help them to function well and to give the greatest enjoyment to everyone. So it is with angling and angling clubs.

By joining a club you not only meet other keen anglers and learn how to fish expertly, but you also learn about certain local fishing rules which you must carefully obey. One of the most important rules concerns the 'closed' season. During this period, usually March to June, no coarse fishing at all is allowed in certain inland waters. This is because the fish are spawning and so must not be disturbed.

Clubs hold regular fishing matches in which members compete against each other, the prizes going to the anglers with the greatest weight of fish over a given period of time. Walk quietly along the waterside at the weekend and you will see anglers seated at regularly spaced intervals. By each angler's feet, and dipping well down into the water, will be a large net. This is the angler's 'keep net'. In this the caught fish are kept. The fish are weighed and then returned, alive, to the water.

You can learn a great deal by watching one of these anglers, but you must be quiet and still or you will frighten the fish away, and then you will not be very popular!

However, perhaps you would rather be a lone fisherman, preferring to get away from everyone and matching your skill against the fish alone, whilst at the same time enjoying the interest of the wild life around you.

This is the joy of angling—you can enjoy it in the company of others, or you can be a lone wolf and not be thought unsociable or peculiar.

Your Equipment

It is not the angler with the most expensive equipment who catches the most or the best fish. Skill, understanding of the conditions of the waters and the fish, plus patience and a little luck, will produce more rewarding results than the finest shop-bought rod and tackle.

Many of the greatest anglers began with a simple garden cane with a nylon line tied to the notched end or held along it by a few small curtain rings bound to the cane—and using a bent pin as a hook. You can also start in this way if you wish, but instead of a bent pin, buy a few hooks from the fishing-tackle shop.

Eyed hooks—hooks with a small ring in the end to which is tied the reel line—are the cheapest.

Hooks are made in a range of numbered sizes, the largest hook bearing the lowest number. These can be bought separately or in packets of assorted sizes. The most useful sizes for a beginner are Nos. 8, 10 and 12.

With a home-made rod and line, plus a few shop-bought hooks, a beginner can make a start and so discover the strange thrill of the long, hopeful, quiet wait. Once the would-be angler has discovered this, he or she is truly 'hooked' as securely as any fish. Then will be the time to think of buying better equipment.

HOOK SIZES

The Rod

When you first enter a fishing-tackle shop, you will see an almost bewildering array of rods of all sizes and colours, and for all types of fishing. It is wise to have in mind the type of rod you need.

If you are going float fishing for coarse fish, mainly in still or quietly flowing waters, you must ask to see light rods for float fishing or general 'bottom-fishing', which is another term for this type of fishing.

Most rods are three-jointed, and are still made from the traditional materials such as split cane, Spanish reed, bamboo or lancewood. The top joint of the better rods will be made of fibreglass. It is advisable to spend a little extra money to obtain a rod with this fibre-glass top joint, as anglers have proved that these are stronger, do not bend, and wear well under all weather conditions.

Rods are also made of tubular steel. These are light, strong and easy to handle, but are more expensive.

A good rod will last for years if well cared for, so it is wise to buy the best quality you can afford. Do not be tempted by the low-priced 'bargains', or the short rods labelled 'for the beginner' or 'boy's rod'. Also beware of the highly-varnished or brightly-painted rod. They *look* attractive, but flash in the sunlight and scare away the fish. A 'flashy-looking' rod is always suspect. Always look for good workmanship and materials, not gaudiness.

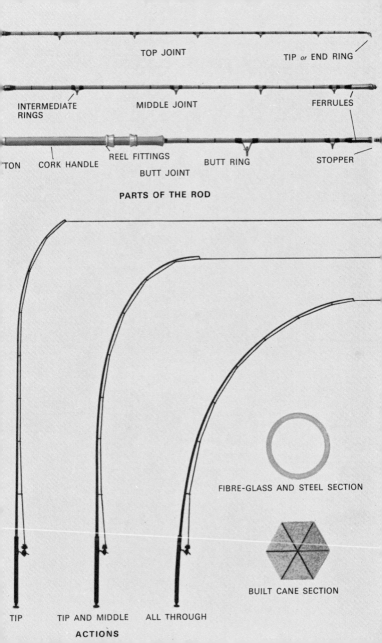

TOP JOINT

TIP *or* END RING

INTERMEDIATE RINGS

MIDDLE JOINT

FERRULES

TON

CORK HANDLE

REEL FITTINGS

BUTT RING

STOPPER

BUTT JOINT

PARTS OF THE ROD

FIBRE-GLASS AND STEEL SECTION

BUILT CANE SECTION

TIP

TIP AND MIDDLE

ALL THROUGH

ACTIONS

Reel, Line and Nets

A fixed-spool reel is the correct type to buy for float-fishing. One of the cheaper models will give you excellent service if you keep it clean and well-oiled.

Your line, which is wound onto the reel, should be made of nylon. Your dealer will sell you a full line; one with a three pounds breaking strain is a good average strength.

A landing net is essential to lift the catch out of the water. It protects the struggling fish from further damage and safeguards your line from breaking. Nylon line is strong, but it *will* break if you happen to catch a larger fish than that intended for your line. Never buy a line thicker than is needed for general use, as the thicker the line in the water, the more suspicious will the fish become—and a suspicious fish is a wary one, and unlikely to take your bait, however tempting it may be.

If you are going in for match fishing you will need a keep net. This is sunk into the water and must be large enough to allow your catch to move and breathe freely. Do not try to economise by buying a small one, for should you make a good catch, the fish will be too crowded and will die.

Even if you are not taking part in match fishing, you should use a keep net if you wish to keep your catch for any length of time to show other people. However, as few coarse fish are good to eat, it is wiser to return them to the water unharmed.

Never leave a fish to pant its life away. This is cruel and unnecessary. It is important to watch and learn how to remove the hook from the fish's mouth without harming it more than necessary. A useful gadget to help you with this, particularly for large fish, is called a disgorger, but great care is needed when using it.

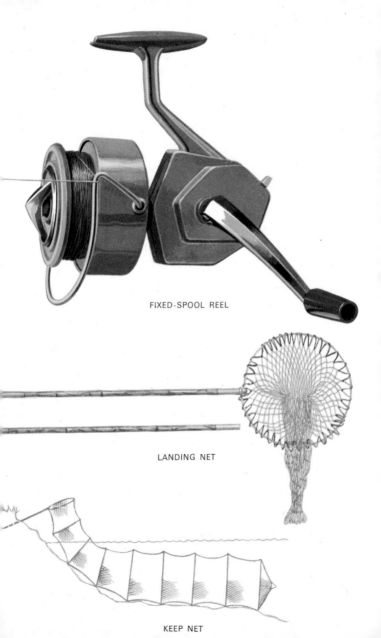

FIXED-SPOOL REEL

LANDING NET

KEEP NET

Floats

Non-fishermen often think that a float is used solely to indicate when a fish is taking the bait. Certainly it indicates this, and part of the excitement is in watching the float for the first signs that a fish is nibbling. However, the main use for a float is to suspend and support the bait at whatever depth the fish are feeding.

The depth at which fish feed depends on the species, the depth of water and its flow. So more than one size and type of float are needed.

In still or slow-moving water, a light float is sufficient. You can make your own from a bird quill, or buy one ready-made. Porcupine quills are also sold as light-weight floats. Sometimes a strong wind will cause even the calmest water to ruffle badly, and if your float is bobbing wildly up and down, a change of float is necessary. If the float is bobbing erratically, the bait suspended below the surface will also be behaving unnaturally, and no fish will try to take food which is acting in this way. So for these conditions you will need an antenna float. This you will have to buy as it is specially designed to withstand wind-ruffled water.

Floats for use in fast-flowing or rough waters are bigger and heavier, but even so these must not be heavier than conditions warrant. If, when a fish is eating the bait, it feels resistance from a too-heavy float, then it will quickly spit out the food and your catch is lost.

You can also buy an anti-wind float for use in running water. This has a round body without a stem, so that it sits low in the water.

Opposite: A. Porcupine quill float.
B. Antenna float.
C. Floats for use in fast running or rough waters.
D. Anti-wind floats for use in running water.

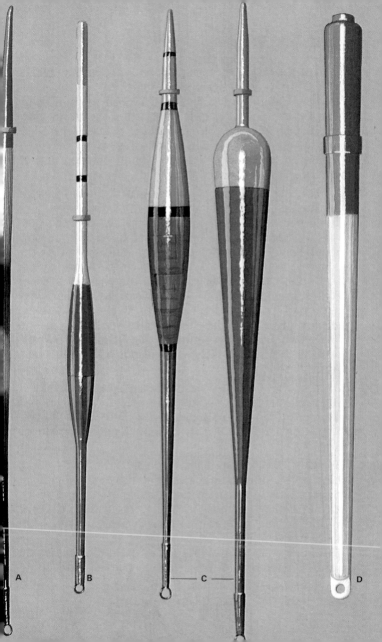

A   B   C   D

Casts and Weights

Eyed hooks are the cheapest, but you can buy hooks which are already whipped. 'Whipped' is the term used for a hook with a length of looped nylon already tied to it. This nylon is finer than the main line, but it is not tied to your main line. Between the hook length and the main line comes the 'cast'. This cast should be of a thickness and strength between that of the hook-length and the main line.

There are two important reasons for these different thicknesses. First, you must have the least thickness of nylon below the water in order to allay the fish's suspicions. Secondly, if the hook and lower line become entangled in weeds or some underwater object, then the breaking point will be at the weakest part—which will be by the hook, which in turn is the cheapest part of your equipment. Better to lose a few hooks than your float and perhaps the rod. By having this weaker, thinner nylon at the hook end, you may lose a promising fish or two, but at least you will have the thrill of a nibble, which you will not get with a thick, clumsy-looking line.

To make your own casts, buy a spool of nylon at slightly less breaking strain than that of your reel line. Cut a yard length and make a small loop at both ends, using the Double Overhand Loop Knot described on Page 40.

Weights—Split Shot. These are shot-gun pellets which have been almost split in half. They are *pinched onto the cast* to make the baited hook hang low in the water, and to make your float 'cock'. Without them the float would lie flat on the water, and a fish pulling on the bait attached to it would feel the resistance and be suspicious. A cocked float glides easily down into the water when pulled, *and* shows you when the fish is biting.

The illustrations opposite show also the use of split-shot when 'ledgering'—i.e. fishing from the bottom.

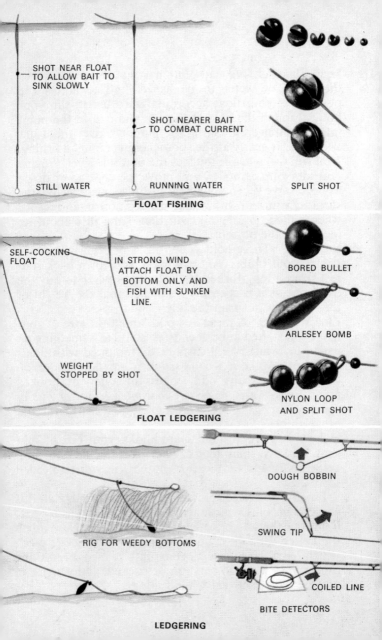

SHOT NEAR FLOAT TO ALLOW BAIT TO SINK SLOWLY

SHOT NEARER BAIT TO COMBAT CURRENT

STILL WATER

RUNNING WATER

SPLIT SHOT

FLOAT FISHING

SELF-COCKING FLOAT

IN STRONG WIND ATTACH FLOAT BY BOTTOM ONLY AND FISH WITH SUNKEN LINE.

WEIGHT STOPPED BY SHOT

BORED BULLET

ARLESEY BOMB

NYLON LOOP AND SPLIT SHOT

FLOAT LEDGERING

RIG FOR WEEDY BOTTOMS

DOUGH BOBBIN

SWING TIP

COILED LINE

BITE DETECTORS

LEDGERING

Oddments

Lead Plummet. A lead plummet enables you to know the depth of water to be fished, and to adjust the position of your float accordingly. To use it, slip your hook through the hole at the top and embed the point into the inset cork. Swing the plummet over the water and lower it *gently* at the spot where you intend fishing. You will feel when it touches the bottom. Keep the line taut, draw up carefully, and move the float up or down as necessary. When your float just disappears below the surface, you will know that its position is correct as, when baited, your hook will then hang just about an inch from the bottom.

Rod-rests. These hold your rod in position when you stretch your limbs. You can make your own back rod-rest from a long forked stick, but it is wiser to buy the front one as it is specially shaped so that the weight of the rod does not trap the line.

Line Winders. A piece of wood, about the size of your hand and slotted at both ends, is useful as something on which to wind several casts ready mounted with floats and shot. Make a second, slightly smaller winder on which to wind any odd lengths of nylon or hooked nylon lines. *Never leave any unwanted hooks or bits of nylon on the banks*—they are a great danger to birds and other animals.

A tin is useful to hold spare hooks, your box of split shot, scissors, small pair of pliers for pinching on shot, extra floats and disgorger. Another tin will be needed for bait.

Finally, you need something in which to carry all this equipment, plus your lunch. Any bag will do as a start; if it is one that can be carried on your shoulders, so much the better. One day you may possess an angler's creel, which is a large wicker box into which everything except your rod and nets can be packed, and which can also be used as a seat while fishing.

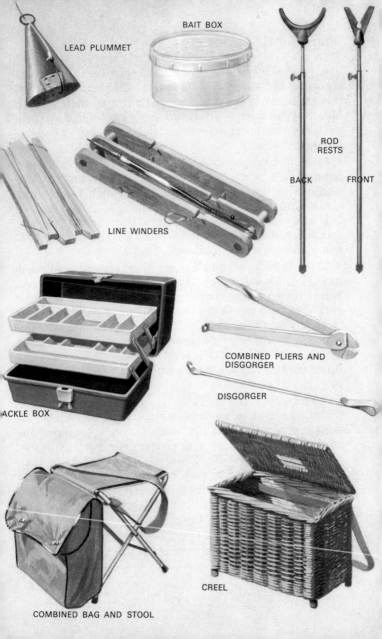

LEAD PLUMMET

BAIT BOX

ROD RESTS

BACK

FRONT

LINE WINDERS

ACKLE BOX

COMBINED PLIERS AND DISGORGER

DISGORGER

COMBINED BAG AND STOOL

CREEL

Fish Identification

A good angler must be able to identify the fish caught. He must know the types of water different species of fish are likely to inhabit, and something of their way of life. But first he must have some knowledge of fish anatomy, in order to understand why they must be handled carefully.

Fish are cold-blooded, which means they have a body temperature which adjusts to the temperature of the water. They breathe by taking in, through the mouth, water containing oxygen and passing it through their gills and out under the gill covers. Because the gills are specially constructed to extract the oxygen *from water*, fish suffocate when lifted out of water.

Sight, taste, smell and feel senses are all well developed in most fresh-water fish. But, like all animals, some see better than others, some have a keener sense of taste and some are more sensitive to vibration. Most fish have a visible 'lateral line', a line containing organs which are in direct contact with the complex nervous system, and which acts as a fish's 'radar' in that it picks up vibrations in the surrounding water and helps a fish to judge its position.

Scales cover the fish's body for protection. These scales are usually covered with a layer of slime—an added protection against parasites and bacterial infection. It is this slime which makes the fish so slippery and difficult to handle. However, you must learn how to hold a fish firmly and yet gently, because if you damage the scaly, slippery covering, and then return the fish to the water, it is likely to pick up some fungoid disease through the damaged parts.

Fish propel themselves by the movements of body and tail. The fins, particularly the tail fin, act as rudders and stabilisers. The shape of the fins is most important for identification.

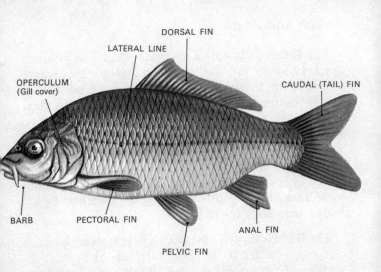

DORSAL FIN

LATERAL LINE

OPERCULUM
(Gill cover)

CAUDAL (TAIL) FIN

BARB

PECTORAL FIN

ANAL FIN

PELVIC FIN

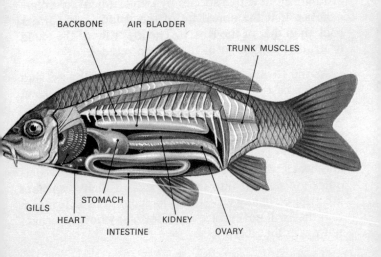

BACKBONE

AIR BLADDER

TRUNK MUSCLES

GILLS

STOMACH

HEART

INTESTINE

KIDNEY

OVARY

COMMON CARP

Roach and Rudd

The Roach is common to most waters, so you will quickly become familiar with its handsome appearance and somewhat shy habits. The larger fish tend to keep to the bottom of the water and are timid in their approach to any bait. Some fish snatch at bait and you know by the violent bobbing or disappearance under water of your float that you have a bite. This is not so with the Roach found in still or slow-running water—it sucks deliberately at the bait, and if you are not watching your float keenly you will miss your catch and be left with a bare hook in the water!

The Rudd is very like the Roach in general appearance, but much bolder in its habits. It feeds at or near the surface of the water, also near the banks, so is more often seen than the Roach.

Despite their similar shape and colouring, you can distinguish these two species by two distinctive pointers —notice that the dorsal fin of the Rudd is set farther back than that of the Roach. The lower lip of the Rudd protrudes, while that of the Roach recedes.

As the Roach is a bottom-feeder, you will need shot on your cast. Try fishing for the Rudd without shot, just letting the bait sink slowly and naturally in the water. With all surface-feeding fish, it is essential to take extra care not to disturb the surface of the water more than you can help, both when casting out the line and when you have your first catch. Surface-feeders quickly disappear into deeper waters if their suspicions are aroused in any way. If this happens, it usually means that they will not surface again for many hours, perhaps not again that day.

RUDD

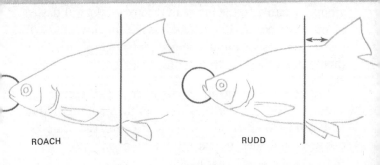

ROACH

RUDD

ROACH

Chub and Dace

Chub and Dace are mainly river fish and, like the Roach and the Rudd, are often mistaken for each other. However, if you look at the shape of the fins you will see that the dorsal and anal fins of the Dace are concave, whereas those of the Chub are convex.

When fully grown, the Chub is a big fish and a fighter when hooked. It snatches at the bait, so an angler knows immediately when he has a bite. But beware, for the Chub has a liking for the overgrown parts of the water along the bank, so the moment it senses danger it dashes at once for cover. It must be played quickly or it will twine the cast around some underwater obstruction; then you will lose both fish and cast.

Young Chub swim in shoals near the surface of the water, but when older they develop their solitary habits and swim alone. In Germany it is called the scale-fish because the scales are exceptionally large.

The Dace is smaller and slighter in build, and will swim in shoals near the surface of the water at all stages of its life. These shoals are fun to watch as they seem to be playing a wonderful game of 'over and under' with each other, then suddenly one will surprise you by leaping up to snatch at a midge or some other small insect on or above the surface of the water.

The head is small by comparison with many other species, so the eyes look especially large and handsome. Like the Chub, the Dace also snatches at the bait.

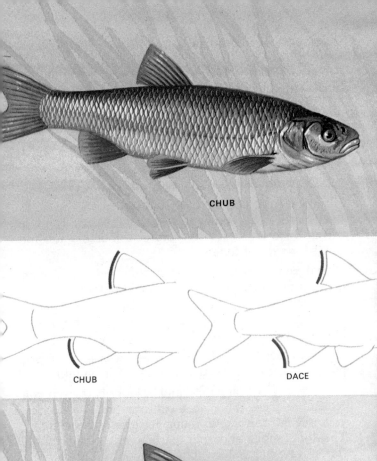

CHUB

CHUB

DACE

DACE

Gudgeon and Barbel

The Gudgeon is found in most rivers, swimming in shoals. Although it is small, it is one of the few coarse fishes which are really good to eat.

To attract fish to your fishing territory it is usual to throw into the water a handful of ground-bait. However, this is rarely necessary with Gudgeon. An old fisherman's trick to bring these inquisitive, sharp-eyed little fish closer is to stir up the bottom of the water with the end of a stick—not too vigorously but just enough to cause small particles of matter to rise in the water. The fish will at once start exploring the discoloured water for suitable scraps of food.

Gudgeon seem to be more greedy and stupid than many of the other species. Once you have found a shoal, the others will stay around and go on taking as much fresh bait as you wish to cast among them, no matter how many you pull out.

Notice that the Gudgeon has *two* barbels, or feelers, protruding from the area at the side of its mouth.

The Barbel is a larger fish and has four barbels. If you remember these differences between the two species, you will not mistake a young Barbel for a Gudgeon. The long snout and four barbels are suited to the Barbel's feeding habits. It swims about on the bottom with its nose in the mud, grubbing out worms and molluscs.

The Barbel cannot live in still or polluted waters, and is only found in clean, fast-flowing rivers. It is a powerful fighter when hooked and, as the weight of a full-grown fish may be 10 lbs. or more, it must be fished for with a strong line and a strong arm.

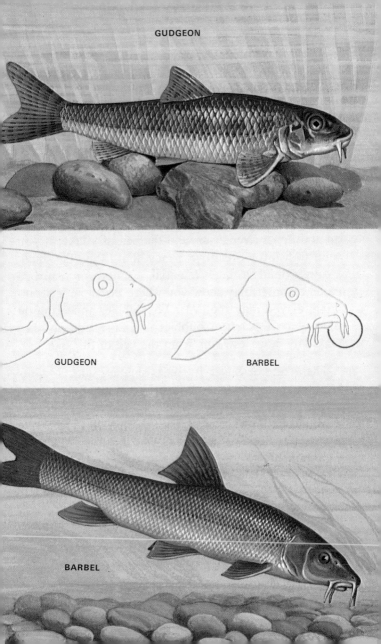

GUDGEON

GUDGEON   BARBEL

BARBEL

Bream

The Common or Bronze Bream is one of the easiest fish to play in most still waters. Once hooked, it seems to accept the inevitable and rarely puts up a fight, although of course it will pull heavily on the line for a while, as do all fish. It feeds on the bottom and, when feeding, stands on its head to rout out the food it prefers. Notice its deep body and you will realise why it has to feed in this upside-down fashion.

Bream swim in shoals, a large shoal travelling slowly up and down river or around the bed of a lake. If you want to fish for Bream, you must first locate the shoal. Heavy ground baiting is essential. A muddy or disturbed patch of water may show you where the shoal is swimming, or you may spot a trail of bubbles appearing on the water. A *patch* of bubbles is a false sign, as they may only be gases rising from the bed of the lake.

The White or Silver Bream is smaller, but its habits are similar. It is not easy to identify a White Bream from a young Common Bream. The only sure way is to count the number of branched rays on the anal fin. The White Bream usually has less than twenty-three rays, the Common Bream more.

Both species are generally covered in an exceptionally thick layer of protective slime. It drips off as they are netted from the water and covers everything the fish contacts. After Bream fishing it is essential to wash and dry all your tackle thoroughly or the smell will linger for days.

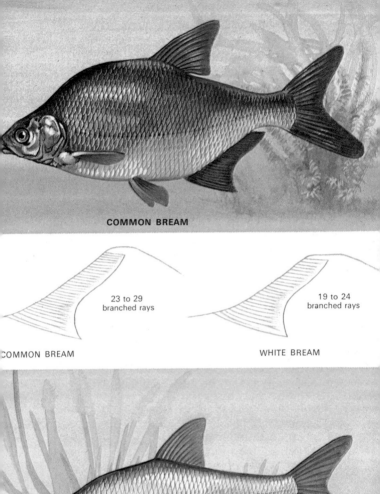

COMMON BREAM

23 to 29 branched rays

19 to 24 branched rays

COMMON BREAM

WHITE BREAM

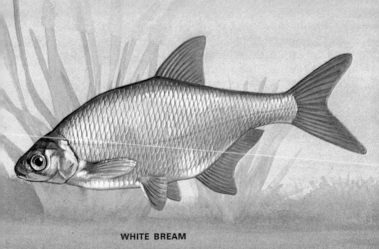

WHITE BREAM

Perch

The Perch is not only the most handsome fish in British waters—it is also one of the easiest to catch because it is exceptionally greedy! Perch swim in shoals, but as a rule the smaller ones swim together and apart from the larger fish. If you hook a small one only a few ounces in weight, it is no use anticipating that your next bite in that area will be a record five-pounder. Five pounds is about the maximum weight, but few grow to this size. Where Perch are breeding, there are usually so many of them that the food supply is not enough for all of them to develop to full size.

Perch like quiet waters and, provided there is sufficient depth, they will gather in large numbers against walls, lock-gates and among submerged tree roots. Once a Perch spots the bait, it will rush and gobble it down before realising the danger. It does not stop to nibble gently—as do Roach and Rudd. It will, of course, blow out the food and suck it in again, perhaps more than once. Most fish do this, so when your float begins to bob *do not* try to pull in at once. Wait until the float disappears below the surface before feeling sure that the fish has really taken the bait, complete with hook.

Inside the mouth of all fish is a mass of cartilage like soft, rubbery tissue. It is not flesh as we know it. This tissue varies in toughness in the different species of fish. In the Perch's mouth it is soft and the hook easily slips out. That is why you must allow the fish to take the bait well into its mouth before attempting to land your bite.

Play your catch gently but firmly. Perch are fighters. If you lose your catch, or even if it pulls the line out of your control, it will warn the rest of the shoal. This will mean the end of your Perch fishing expedition for the day.

A TWO POUND
PERCH

PERCH

Carp and Tench

Both these fish live in the still, weedy waters of ponds and lakes. There is little chance of catching either during the winter months; the Carp eats very little during the winter, so will not take the bait, and the Tench hibernates for long periods in the mud at the bottom.

Many anglers consider the Carp to be the most intelligent of all fish and, therefore, the hardest to catch. It is one of the largest, weighing anything up to thirty or more pounds, and is a strong fighter. Strong tackle is needed, but if this is too thick or obvious-looking then the knowing Carp, with its keen eyesight, will be suspicious and keep away. The bait must fully cover the hook, or the Carp will *never* swallow it.

You must be prepared for long, silent and motionless waits when Carp fishing. The slightest sound or vibration from the bank or on the water—even the passing of a shadow over the water—will warn them off.

There are several varieties of Carp, some of them distinguishable by their scales. The Common Carp (illustrated on Page 21) is fully scaled. The Mirror Carp has few scales, but these are large and mirror-like in appearance. Most of the Mirror Carp's scales are arranged in a set pattern—in an uninterrupted line along the lateral line, with just a few in groups on the rest of the toughened skin. The Leather Carp has even less scales, and these are thinly scattered over its thick, leathery skin.

Tench do not grow as large as Carp, and tend to feed more on the bottom of the water. Early morning and late evening are the best times to tempt them to the bait. However, the Tench is not a nice fish to eat, whereas the Carp is, so it is a fish to be caught for recording purposes only.

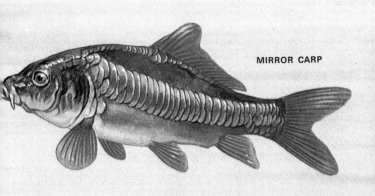

MIRROR CARP

LEATHER CARP

TENCH

'Small Fry'

The Bleak and Ruffe are two small river fishes only a few inches long. Many anglers regard them as a nuisance, as they steal the bait intended for larger fish.

The Bleak swims in silvery shoals at the surface of the water, and is easily caught with a small hook baited only a few inches below a float. If you wish to get rid of a shoal of Bleak in order to fish for other species lower down, it is a good idea to throw a piece of bread into the water. At once they will mob it and drift downstream with it.

The Ruffe, or Pope, lurks at the bottom of the water and nibbles at any bait within sight. Many an angler has wound in his line hopefully . . . only to find on the end a tiny three-inch fish rather like a small Perch in appearance, but lacking its glorious colour. However, the Ruffe, like the Gudgeon, is tasty to eat, so it is sometimes worthwhile catching a few.

Even smaller is the Minnow, the 'tiddler' of net and jam-jar days. If you want to catch a few Minnows to examine them closely, or for a garden pond, lower a glass bottle baited with bread into the water. To the top of the bottle should be fastened a length of string. After a while pull up the bottle, and if there are Minnow in the water then some will certainly be in your bottle.

Sticklebacks, Loaches and Miller's Thumbs are other 'small fry' you will see as you fish for larger species. Tiny, yes, but not to be despised, as they are as perfect in their construction and as interesting in their habits as the larger fish.

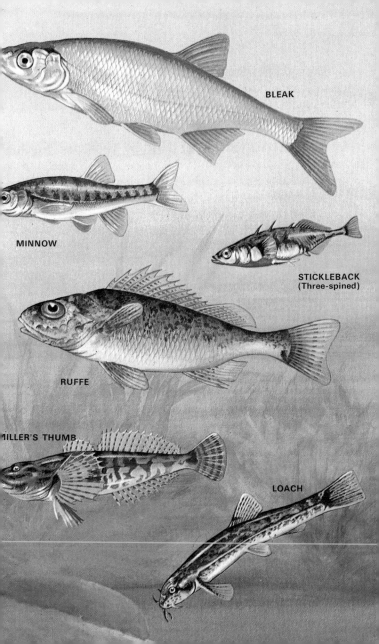

BLEAK

MINNOW

STICKLEBACK
(Three-spined)

RUFFE

MILLER'S THUMB

LOACH

Eels

Every angler meets the Eel again and again on his fishing expeditions. Eels can be a nuisance, especially the smaller ones, as they can tangle a cast and line into a dreadful state.

As a rule it is the smaller ones, the 'bootlaces', which are most likely to be hooked during daylight. The larger ones usually feed at night, staying hidden during daylight. However, all are bottom feeders and rarely take any type of vegetarian bait. If you avoid using live-bait you are less likely to be troubled by them.

However, if one is hooked, then the following is the least troublesome way to deal with it: do not use your net and do not dangle the Eel in the air or lay it down on the grass. Instead draw it to the water's edge and drag it gently onto the bank. If there is some stonework or brickwork close by, drag it onto this. If not, spread newspaper on the ground. On such surfaces it will lie quietly enough for you to remove the hook. It will not lie quietly on grass or mud, but will wriggle, writhe and twist, taking your cast and line with it until everything is in such a slimy tangle that you can do nothing more than gather it all into a ball ready for the dustbin when you get home.

Large Eels are good to eat. If you catch one and want to eat it for supper, you must either kill it right away or put it into a sack. Eels are one of the few fishes which can breathe out of water and if you leave one lying on the bank, it will quickly slither away into hiding and eventually back into the water.

Bait

Many anglers use live-bait, such as worms or maggots, for luring the larger fish to the hook. But live-bait is not necessary for the smaller fish; bread will do just as well, if you prepare it properly.

You can use bread as it is, cutting it into cubes of various sizes, or making a paste. Paste must be firm, especially for fishing in running water, but it must not be rock hard. Put some stale bread into a clean rag and dip it into water until fully soaked through. Squeeze all the water out and then knead the paste in your hands, mixing in a little raw flour as you do so. The flour helps to firm the paste.

You can experiment by colouring and flavouring the paste. Custard powder instead of flour will turn it yellow. Cheese tempts some fish, honey others, particularly Carp. Potato, partly boiled and unskinned, makes another good bait for Carp. Stewed wheat, seed barley, macaroni, bacon rind, elderberries and cherries when in season can all be tried. Stewed hempseed is excellent for Roach, but it is forbidden in some waters as fish have been overfed with it.

GROUND-BAIT. It is no use casting your line into any water unless you know there are some fish about. Use ground-bait to lure them to your area. This should be a small handful of suitable food, previously well soaked to make it sink quickly, and then scattered loosely into the water. Ground-bait is not always needed in lakes and ponds, but it is usually necessary in rivers. Again, dried bread crushed or put through the mincer can be used. If you have any other cereal foods available, such as ground rice, semolina or bran, then add some to the bread, as these will help to make the bait even more tempting. When casting your ground-bait into a flowing river, first mould it into a fairly large ball and cast it *upstream* of your intended fishing position.

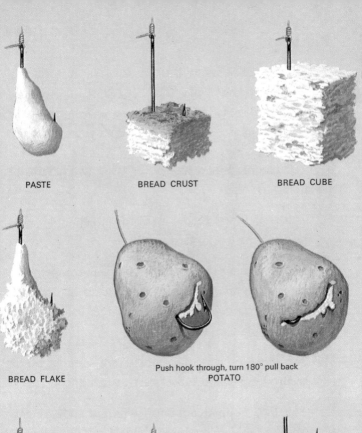

PASTE

BREAD CRUST

BREAD CUBE

BREAD FLAKE

Push hook through, turn 180° pull back
POTATO

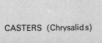

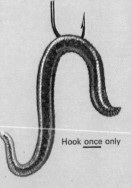

Hook <u>once</u> only

MAGGOT

CASTERS (Chrysalids)

WORM

Knots

Nylon is tricky material to tie *securely*; an ordinary thumb or reef knot will *not* do. It is essential to learn the following knots before beginning to fish, otherwise you will lose more casts and hooks than you can afford.

1. The Double Blood Knot—for tying two lengths of nylon together.

2. The Half Blood Knot—used for attaching an eyed hook to the line or cast.

3. The Whipping or Domhof Knot—a stronger knot for joining an eyed hook to a thicker line or cast, generally used when fishing for larger fish. Also for tying spade-end hooks.

4. The Double Overhand Loop Knot—for making a secure loop at the end of cast or reel line.

5. The Two Loops Knot—for joining a hook already attached to a nylon looped hook-length to a looped reel line, or two loops on cast and line. Pass the cast loop over the reel loop. Bring the hook up through the reel loop and pull the two loops together tightly.

When your knots have been pulled tightly, always cut off projecting ends neatly.

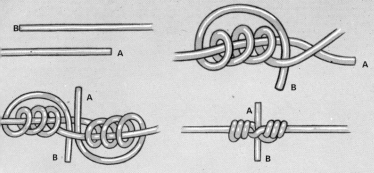

THE DOUBLE BLOOD KNOT

THE HALF BLOOD KNOT

THE WHIPPING or DOMHOF KNOT

THE DOUBLE OVERHAND LOOP KNOT

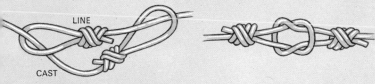

TWO LOOPS KNOT

Fishing Technique

You are now about to pit your wits against Nature. All wild things are suspicious of everything and everyone—they have to be in order to survive at all, so the first important thing to remember is—don't frighten the fish or you will never make a catch.

Approach the water's edge stealthily and quietly; if there is any shelter—bushes or rushes—make use of them. If there are no sheltering objects to hide behind, try to choose a position immediately in front of a bush, tree or tall grass. Fish are used to seeing the outlines of such objects against the sky-line, so will then not notice you if you keep still. Keep low, sit to fish rather than stand, and prepare your tackle back from the water's edge.

Movement scares off fish, so does *vibration*. You will remember the *lateral* line on the fish's body, described on Page 20; it is this line of sensory nerves which pick up the vibrations of your footsteps on the bank, or of the bag dumped heavily down.

A shadow cast on the water will also scare off fish. It is, therefore, necessary to watch the position of the sun. If it is behind you as you approach the water, keep as low as possible and keep your rod low, too.

Having reached a good fishing position, do not be in a hurry to cast your line. Sit perfectly still for a while and watch the waters. In spite of your careful approach you may have aroused some suspicions, so give the fish time to gain confidence once more.

Observe these simple rules and you will become a successful angler. You will also gain many wonderful glimpses of wild birds and animals. Such glimpses only come to the person who is prepared to keep still and quiet for long periods—the perfect angler, in fact.

Float Fishing

You have chosen your spot which we will assume is by still water and are now ready to assemble your tackle. Keep out of sight of the water when you do this. Next set up the rod-rests and then put your rod together, having previously lightly greased the ferrules. Check carefully that the rings through which your line passes are in line with each other from butt to tip. Next attach the reel and see that the running line is lightly greased with line-dressing, a tin of which can be bought from a dealer.

Thread the line through the rings, bringing about six feet through the top ring. Lay your rod on the rod-rests to do this and the rest of your assembly work, as any dust or grit on the reel will foul the line and mechanism.

Your hook will already be tied to your cast—you will have prepared several of these at home, complete with split-shot. One shot will probably be sufficient if you are fishing in still waters. Slip your float onto the line and tie your cast to the line, using a Two Loops Knot, as both ends should be ready looped.

Next, if the stretch of water is new to you, you must plumb the depth, using your plummet as explained on Page 18. Do this as quietly as possible, avoiding splashing or disturbing the water.

Having adjusted your float, pull out your cast and bait the hook. Throw a little ground-bait into the water, and cast your line in after it. With a fixed-spool reel, casting is a simple action and nearly always accurate.

Now wait a while. If nothing happens, gently wind in and check the bait. It may need renewing. Cast again and watch carefully . . . suddenly your float dips—it is pulled under. You have a bite!

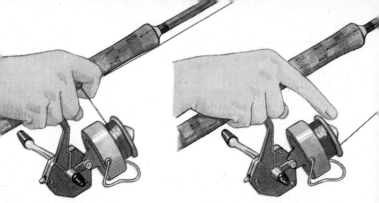

rior to casting, with the
ne trapped between forefinger
nd butt and the bale arm open.

During the cast, the line released
and the finger in a position to slow it
down if necessary by brushing
against it. After the cast a turn of
the handle closes the bale arm

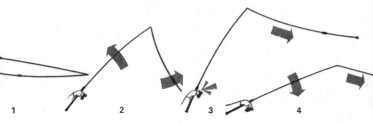

UNDERHAND CAST (for accuracy)

. Hold the cast just above the bait with your free hand and point the rod at the spot where you
ish your bait to land. **2.** Sharply raise the rod, at the same time releasing the cast. **3.** When the
ait reaches the limit of its outward swing release the line trapped by your finger. **4.** Slowly lower
e rod to point at the bait as it enters the water.

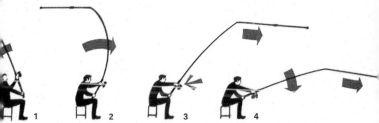

OVERHEAD CAST (for greater distance)

Hold the rod with both hands and bring it back over your shoulder. **2.** Whip the rod forward.
Release the line when the bait reaches its outward limit. (The timing of the release is crucial and
ll need practice). **4.** Lower the rod to follow the bait towards the water.

Your First Bite

When you have a bite, keep calm! If you are excited, you will lose control of your rod and line. Hold the rod well up (Fig. 1)—never let the tip dip towards the water. Your rod acts as a spring and should help you to play the fish. If you drop the tip of your rod towards the water, you are wrongly playing the fish on the line itself.

Wind in carefully, but do not *lift* the fish clear of the water on the line or allow it to splash about on the surface. A fish struggling underwater does not seem to worry unduly the other fish round about, but anything splashing *on* the water will scare them all away, and you will catch no more fish in that section of the water.

Draw your catch slowly and gently towards the bank. Take your landing net in your left hand, *sink it under the water and guide your fish over the rim* (Fig. 2). This is important. Do not *scoop* the fish. Bring the fish over the submerged net and, once it is over, raise the net quickly but smoothly (Fig. 3).

If you have a keep net, you remove the hook and slip your fish carefully into the net. If you have no keep net, remove the hook as gently and quickly as you can (Fig. 4). Remember that your fish is choking and suffocating so long as it is out of water. If you wish to measure or weight it, do so as quickly as you can and then gently *slip* it back into the water (Fig. 5). *Do not throw it in.*

You will find it helpful to keep an old cotton glove or piece of cloth with your tackle. This can be put on when handling slippery fish and will give you a surer grip.

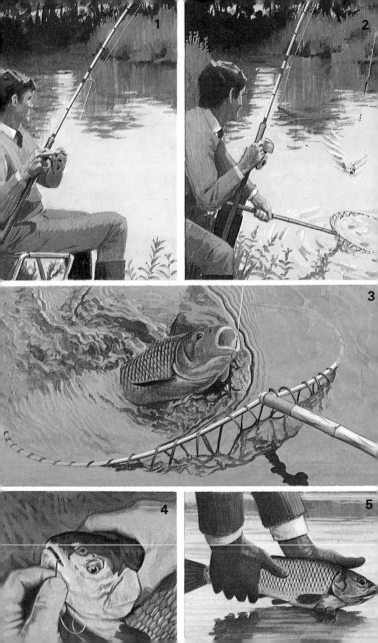

The Angler's Responsibility

An angler must help to maintain the stock of fish in the water, so that other fishermen can enjoy their sport. He does this in several ways: by returning fish alive and undamaged to the water; by joining a local club and paying his membership fee regularly so that the club has enough money to spend on restocking club waters when necessary; by looking after the interests generally of all anglers; and by teaching all newcomers how to fish and how to respect the rules of the sport.

Always respect other people's property, and never force your way through a wire fence or hedge. Never take a short cut *across* a field unless you have permission. Always use the proper path. Do not climb gates if they are made to open—it weakens the hinges. Always shut gates carefully after you.

Pick up every scrap of litter. Not only is it against the law to leave rubbish about, but it leaves an unsightly mess which spoils the pleasure of other people. Be particularly careful to pack up all bottles, tins, plastic bags, hooks and nylon lines. All these can cause serious injury and, all too often, death to cattle, wild life and to humans.

REMEMBER—it only needs one inconsiderate or careless angler to give a bad name to all anglers. Once a farmer has had to pay for damage done on his property, or has lost a good animal through injury, then all privileges he may have granted to local anglers might be withdrawn—perhaps for ever.

Hints and Tips

At the end of a day's fishing, clean and dry all your equipment carefully. This is essential. If you put your rod and tackle away damp and dirty, it will soon be useless to you. It is particularly important to dry your line and, before rewinding, to regrease the parts which have been in the water. Examine rods for damaged varnish and frayed whippings, and renew where necessary. Examine hooks and casts regularly for signs of wear, otherwise too many 'bites' might get away.

Read carefully the rules and conditions printed on your River Board Licence and also the rules of your local club. They are intended to help you and your fellow anglers to get the best out of your chosen sport.

Do not feel ashamed if you return home without having made a catch. Only those who know nothing of the art of fishing call this a failure. The true fisherman knows that there is far more to the sport than the actual act of landing a fish. What this 'more' is you will discover for yourself as the months and years go by.

Finally, do not think you now know all there is to know about fishing; you do not, and you never will! It is a hobby for a life-time, and there is always something new and exciting to learn about the art of fishing, and above all—about the fish themselves.

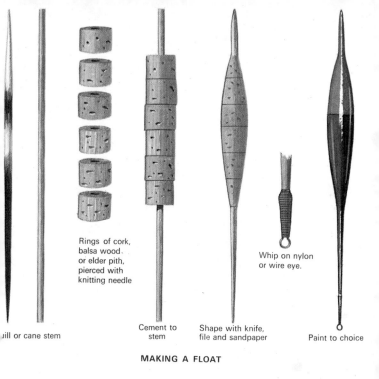

Quill or cane stem

Rings of cork,
balsa wood
or elder pith,
pierced with
knitting needle

Cement to
stem

Shape with knife,
file and sandpaper

Whip on nylon
or wire eye.

Paint to choice

MAKING A FLOAT

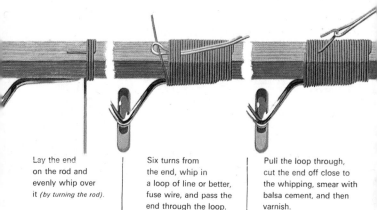

Lay the end
on the rod and
evenly whip over
it *(by turning the rod)*.

Six turns from
the end, whip in
a loop of line or better,
fuse wire, and pass the
end through the loop.

Pull the loop through,
cut the end off close to
the whipping, smear with
balsa cement, and then
varnish.

WHIPPING

INDEX